To Susan
all best wishes
Maggie Harris

FROM BERBICE TO BROADSTAIRS

From Berbice to Broadstairs

Maggie Harris

MANGO PUBLISHING
2006

Published by Mango Publishing, London UK
P.O. Box 13378, London SE27 OZN
email: info@mangoprint.com
website: www.mangoprint.com

ISBN 1 902294 28 9
EAN 9781902294285

British Library Cataloguing in Publication Data
A CIP catalogue record for this book is available from the British Library

Produced by Bookchase printed in the EU

Artwork by Karen O'Connor, cover design by Reggie Freeman

... From Berbice to Broadstairs –
that phosphorescence danced between
a middle passage and a future way ...

'Candlefly'
Ian Dieffenthaler

For my family and all those who have inspired and supported me, especially the Write Women Poetry group, and to Karen O'Connor for the cover design.

Some of these poems have been published in *Agenda*, *Brown Eyes*, *Calabash* (New York University), *Connections*, *Dancing with Words* (Year of the Artist, South East Arts), *The Doghouse Book of Ballads*, *Equinox*, Kent Arts & Libraries Postcards, Microphone On! (The Whitehouse, Limerick), *Poetry Review Newsletter*, *Poetry Wales*, *Poui*, (University of the West Indies), *The Shop*, and *Wasafiri*.

Contents

Time

I trapped time once as he struggled to escape,
trapped him in a fist of wet sand
deceitfully trickling through my fingers.
From the egg in which I crouched, palming pies out of mud
watching pearls of green river ooze like jewels,
rise like bubbles in a pot,
time squatted like a dwarf on my shoulder.
Is it you? They cried:. Come child, come,
it is time that you move from this place to that,
it is time that you left, that you went.

I trapped time once, knotted in the finger of a glove
choked him in the air that I breathed, pure carbon
trembling in a roomful of trees.
I sealed him in a jar of meridian blue,
washed him in a rush of ochre;
deaf to the cries that were rippling –
Come child, come. It is time that you left,
it is time that you move from this place to that,
it is time that you left, that you went.

I trapped time once in a wave of sea water,
banished him far on a reef,
but his voice broke free and sings from the shadows –
Come child, come, it is time that you cease all this running.
For don't you know you will always be mine?
Always, always be mine..

Parakeets

(for Chloe)

They haven't lost their accents – not like me –
their piercing cries ricochet off Joss Bay Road
through bark and leaf, beech, elm

Not for the first time, my heart
flies to meet them, escapees
celebrating their freedom through procreation

We lift you over the puddles, you've got your
school-shoes on; we didn't expect to see you today
it's been so long

Your hands grip the dog's lead tightly, she slows,
knowing it isn't one of us whom she can drag,
yank, dash at the slightest scent into undergrowth.

We walk through the farm, up to the lighthouse.
'I came here once', you say, 'with school'.
Four schools ago, and you're only seven.

But we don't ask questions, just point out
the rows of cabbages, the horses
and the sea bright in the winter sun.

You pick a cabbage leaf to show your new teacher,
find a feather, two; you hand them over
'Put them in the jar at yours', you say, 'with the others.'

On the way back we gather sticks, which Grandad snaps
and places in the carrier for the wood-burner,
while your keen eyes scan the ground.

The parakeets are still there. We rest
on a bench and watch their brilliant lime-green
plumage zing

Later, I realize
I never told you the story about those home-birds.
In fact, I never mentioned Guyana once.

The Berbice River

she sleeping still brown sluggish
like awee wimmin dih men dem sneer
shoving dere pepsi caps clear
off heads awash
with sun and beer

she dutty-brown thighs spread-eagle
she sanctum where she dreaming
strong sistuhs paddling silent
vanishing
in mist and myth

she toes sink
in mud, crabs scuttling,
and through she palm frond fingers
and dih glare
ship come sudden

and hover
some Martian kite
million a silver feet
pon top sea level

they steal she name for planters chairs
for mad houses and promises
thinking she sleeping still

constant lap of lullabies wash she
slapping at she blood-let banks
soothing currents simmering
bubbling up
rib by rib 'long she spine

hushing up woman rage rising
chain and bones clanking
gold tumbling
round she grave

she look like she sleeping

but she ain't.

Mapping

Welcome, body
let me trace you
journey over loose belly, baby belly
knife scar, sizzle kisses
Mummy kisses, Daddy kiss
sugar-cane lash, suckle-baby breast

Long time journey from Madeira
Africa, brake at Goree
confuse at currents and name change
Gold Coast, Accra, Kwakwani, Kent
tree limb splintering
fall in the ink
fall in the water

shell ears listening, remembering
brown-eyed Mama and grey-eyed Dada
rockababy songs on a hammock swinging
to Jim Reeves and Elvis and Satchmo
gospel calling, the Swanee river

parchment and skin
contours rising, falling
lovers roosting, calling
planting kisses on the plateau
soak up in the rainforest

Dr. Ferdinand dimpling his thumbprints on my ass
slap me, lift me, cry me, write me, label
me like a cocktail: 'Mixed.'

birth certificate: 'Mixed.'
pen wobbled on the x
centred me neatly
in limbo

fall in the ink
fall in the water
eyes of blue and heart of steel
darling, how come the golden hair?
some white Bajan
in a Berbice chair

and all the time they rocked me
straightened my nose with their fingers
powdered my skin with Johnsons Baby

some heartbeat was beating
a Senagalese drum rhythm
a Malian harmony
strings and skins I have no name for

missing
missing
missing

and only these anklebones
carry a memory
that has no name

Origins

Yes, track me the scent of my skin on a coast off Paramaribo
where a trade wind blowing its precious cargo
doesn't know that one day they'll build rockets
from behind those trees and aim for the moon
where this captain is sailing his ship by the stars

Trace me that line of ancestors on that shore
Ibo, Hausa. A Madeiran fisherman drawing his nets off a reef
waters that flowed from Chechnya and the Nile
one single ice-flow melting
down from the tundra

I am listening for the soft pad of a footfall morning
a Yamomani and Macusi morning
a grandfathers-who-don't-know-their-name-yet morning
skins melting into ochre forests where young men
are rubbing tinder sticks in the sun
and women drape skins even as you

dropping soft-pawed from the rocks
spine bristling with porcupine quills
into new centuries of prayer flags and eddoes
and turbans mimicking a call

land on the prow of this ship
and watch the Captain as he stares at the stars
thumbing his salt-water map
his wolf-eyes holding the moon

Yes, track me the scent of my skin on a Paramaribo morning
where an archipelago whispering the rosary
calls so enticingly.
But, tread water, wait.
I don't wish to arrive yet, not just yet.

I Am a Guyana Woman

I am a Guyana woman
my mothers rubbed oil
into my skin
sang songs to the slap
of clothes on stone
carried water before the connection
before economics broke the connection

I am a Guyana woman
my English daughters
rub lotions into their skins
recipes stolen from the forest
where rivers run with mercury
seep into ocean floors
economics create pollution

From houses on riversides
children had played
sliding their bodies dirt dry
and mango smooth
into currents cut by canoes
cool water
once pure

I am a Guyana woman
my mothers
rubbed oil into my skin
sang songs to the slap
of clothes on stone

lit candles to lengthen the day
opened books that I should learn
so that I should leave
so that I should always have running water
so that I should never have
to slap my clothes on the stone

O Guyana
my voice is a river
I run
to renew the connection

Poetry

And it was at that moment Poetry arrived
in search of me• Arrived like a new Yamaha
spewing warm dust and stones
up from the unpaved road

It tunnelled into my entrails
like a dybbuk, lassoed me so I fell
was dragged like a grazed steer
bucking on Rupununi plains

It bubbled up from the void
on the front porch where Grand-Daddy voice
rising, chastising, and into the lull
of Miss Moses reciting a passage from *Maud*

It arrived and hoisted my self
into black leatherette and hot steel
kicking rhythms running
outa my Daddy's blues

and a steelpan practising down yard.
It cleaved a way through the stones
and feathers spitting from my throat
into a new me skinned and bleeding

under a South American sun.
Before she came
I was barely there
barely there at all

•from Pablo Neruda, 'Poetry'

**'...the night-time put on
flesh and blackness...'**

Zora Neale Hurston,
Their Eyes Were Watching God

... wearing two-tone shoes and new cotton
he filters an aroma singed with incense and cardamoms
through Demerara shutters
sealed tight against his breath

Inside, the young widow fastens locks
checks under the bed
pats four small heads
kisses the cold cross around her neck

He's on the front-steps tapping
a soft-shoe shuffle into perfumed oleander
and a Lighthouse cigarette.
                    With a step-and-change
the guard-dog howls into a blue moon.

A Day

Morning

and when I return
hold me deep within your breathing
of that very first season
where tamarind and guinep
star-apple and lime
knew our names
and hot-peppered and oiled
our brown skins
to the Praise He! of the Baptists
over Ramlall's fence

Noon

the Angelus bell
will be ringing
and the boy from the grocery store
calls up from downstairs
flushing us out
from beneath our mothers' sheets
into a noon-time
a sun-burning hot-head time
a mango and bird-pepper time
a sitting on the back-steps lime

Afternoon

fresh lemonade
ice cubes melting
my fingers swell from the heat
a hummingbird flits
through the bougainvillea
on the porch, his head
the size of your thumbnail
his wife calls him and he goes
invisible wings faster
than sight

Evening

night drops like a waterfall
spraying us with stars
they stick to our skins
like glow worms
so brief, so brief
then drowning
in that hollow, your neck
swallowing and swallowing
the sting of my mouth
and all those lies

of leaving

To the Bougainvillea

O Belisha, Beloved, my Darling
O beguiling bell-bird of the trades
O bedizened madame of porches
Beldame of window-frames

O My Lady of carmine verandas
My Lady of the canes
O my Darling of planter's rum punches
Clinking of ice in the shade

Begin the beguine by transplanting
The velveteen burr of your pain
By whispering an elegy
An Iliad, of trade winds

And oceans and rains
Of boarding strange ships
With your flushed lips
Your patron's arm on your waist

Belisha, Beloved, my Darling
Survivor of hurricanes
Below you begonias are weeping
In your English benediction of grace

From This Same Veranda

From this same veranda Miss Beaumont order her lime juice
Cool and sweet in the heat
Slow ships roll on the tide

From this same veranda Great-Grandmother runs
Apron full of limes
There's a new breeze on the skyline

From this same veranda Pastor calls my fathers up
No more talking drums, no sunset gatherings
Underneath them limes

From this same veranda Grandmother sweeps new dust
There's a rocking roll in her low-slung hips
And a morning light in her eyes

From this same veranda my mother hold that baby tight
Deep-voices Louis Armstrong, partify the psalms
Whilst

From this same veranda I watch my blue jeans swing
On the washing line, my toenail polish shine
And in no time

It getting crowded up here with fathers and mothers
Sisters and brothers, grand and godmothers
Aunty niece from Toronto, Chicago, Accra
North Island, Berbice, Castries
And Brighton, England

But y'know – there's always room for one more – so
From this same veranda I call my child
Darlin' shove up that rocking chair, come
Join us up here for a lime*

*Liming – hanging out

New Lands, Long Hands

Tragedy had clouded those still young years
that should have brought her pleasure.
Husband, mother, father, country
all gone in the space of a decade.

Snakes and crocodiles slid out of the rivers,
Jumbie man walked the land.
She gathered her daughters
and crossed the skies, said goodbye to Guyana.

In this new land she rolled up her sleeves
shivered at bus-stops, mopped new floors
modified her South American tongue
to curl the English way.

Her home returned to her
through telephone calls and letters
tales of tough times in Guyana
of who was where
who married who
who'd migrated
who was dead.

When she visits, she comes
with carrier bags full of this and that.
'Guyanese people,' she says,
'Never walk with their long hands'.

Imprint
(for Hilary)

She gave me the inkwell she found in the Thames
And here it stands on the windowsill remembering

Voices are uncurling like genies, their stories tumble
Into my century, there is Miss and Mam, and Preacher

They're louder when it rains, it was the rain that shifted
Them free of the mud, though the dredger helped

I'm trying to write my own story, my journey down
Another river, a time swiftly passing and me needing

To chronicle it. This is not a time for slate or chalk
But paper, computers, ink. Why then should a small

Stone jar scream so loudly, and why do I feel this restless
Reach for a feather?

Jugnu Bhangra
(for the bhangra dancers of Gravesend)

It sprang out of the barrel of wood and leapt into the school
hall like a Chinese Dragon
the drummer igniting thunder with his firesticks on taut
goatskin still alive, and dancing
taking the licks into a bass sound screaming from the Punjab
to Gravesend

It licked the feet of the dancing boys
set them alight so they spring from the floor as if burnt
vaulting like young tigers into tree branches of bowed backs,
cupped palms, strong shoulders

Bowed backs, cupped palms, strong shoulders
rippling in the memory of celebration, of harvests freed from
the blood and toil of sweat
the curving of backbones into soil and seed, the turning of
footsteps into factories and warehouses

Along the walls Nike trainers slumber under the shadows of
benches
whilst dancers' feet beat and flail the floor like so many
flagellations
whipped into a frenzy of jubilation by the drum and the dance
master's claps

Feet and drum reverberating, lasering from clap to skin to
ceiling
Bhangra splicing though the concrete walls, the glass roof, the
school playground, the tops of houses
firing a Jugnu* trail of its own, before finding a space, and
settling.

*firefly

In Search of My Fathers
The Powell-Cotton Museum, Birchington

that eye that blinks against the sun's glare
white on the black tip of a parang
is it you?

that bare foot on the sepia ground
toes splayed flat through cobwebbed dust
is it you?

I press my nose to the glass
remembering your smell
but the air conditioning has dried your sweat

you are trapped between glass
and memory, as dry as
the bloodline that curves from this Africa

but I can feel you breathing
in the lift of my own breath
and you're calling

stern as always
my name.

Museum Piece: Ibex

Let me remove your cold eyes from my frenzied dreams
where your re-assembled skin re-awakens its sinews and
blood
Yours are the cries I hear from my linen bed
through a European darkness, where your shit stains
and the smell of fear have been sterilised
and mock me from behind this glass

Science, do I know you, now you've given me the right
to be educated into the markings of a dead Ibex
felled as he was grazing high up in the Simian mountains?

Well I've learned about the Ibex
and how much a native bearer made
and the rate of exchange in 1899

But I can't for the life of me calculate
how many Maria Theresa dollars that makes
or the fact that something

doesn't quite add up.

Cry Me a River

She's out with her Daddy
The back of her coat is tucked in her knickers
Shall I tell them?

I'm rushing to meet you – poetry is on my lips
This is the South Bank, Daddy!
I'm a long way from home.

Dear Claude ...
(for Claude MacKay, and writing women)

Dear Claude,
Your words have reached me late
As I write here in the weald, where some might say I dwell
Within the belly of the beast. Here castles and monuments
Rise like trees, and moats like banded jewels guard and glitter
Oasts, and merchants' dwellings, galleries.
It takes no leap of vision to imagine whole cavalries
Rushing at me through these trees.

'A tiger's tooth', you write, of your adopted Motherland
Where Liberty and Black are whip and glove,
And I remember lashings of the cane
And passages of Pope, but then again
That fast beating of the heart when letters came!

My heart beats still and flutters
A valve, like Demerara shutters, closed to wind and rain
But scents creep in, that thirsty aftertaste of sugarcane.
My eyes rove, whose house, where?
Whose great-grandmother's taste for sugar in her tea
Whose middle son crossed that sea
For hands-on experience in 17th century management?

The sadness is, you are not here to see
Your words like poppy fields enliven, recreate this landscape
Bond me with these friends whose hallelujahs echo mine.
The gladness is, our mistress set us free
The moment she commanded:
Look, at me.

Pancho Villa's Daughter
(for Desiree)

Pancho Villa's daughter
fresh from a continent where blood dries
quickly on the plains
young as a suckling spruce
old as Mayans

scatters Euros now
stacks them neatly in numerical order
behind a glass window
through eyes as grey as the rain

you'd never know it,
behind that glass partition
with its beech trim
and bronzed name-plate

sits a daughter of the plains
trading dollars for escudos
efficiently advising on Tessas, Isas
blue chip files and overseas investments

The South Coast accent
wavers on a trade wind
ushered briskly through the swing doors
as dry as the yucca straining

for a square of blue.
But don't talk to her of open spaces

of savannahs rippling
like land eels in the heat;

don't talk to her of
vaqueros voiceless as vagrants
with 1969 on a movie screen.

Her face will shut as swiftly as a time lock
will look past you as cold
as the morning rain.

1961

(for Yonnette)

aeroplanes were a rarity then
crossed our skies maybe once a week
we stood at that front gate in St John Street
three curly haired children
pointing upwards
shouting Aeroplane!
jumping up and down
at the silver bird flying south to Brazil
north to the islands

Where do planes go?
What do they bring?
Babies, my mother said
leaning on the porch, head upturned
rubbing half-circles on her belly
with one slow hand

So each week we shouted
Aeroplane! Aeroplane!
Please to bring us a baby!
and so it came to pass
the dipping of wings
a cry from the bedroom
you my baby sister
shine head same colour
as fuselage in sunlight
so in black and white photos you glow
with a halo

Eliza

(In response to Gillian Allnut's poem, 'Alien')

Always spinning she was
that Eliza.

Weavin an spinnin
pinnin an tuckin

scissoring through paper patterns
with pictures they brung her

from *Movie News* and
Hollywood Today.

From dawn
in below-stairs gloom

pinheads diamante like stars
prickled whole tiaras

of wish dreams into the loom
of her fingers,

whilst above stairs
the whistling struggled

to find the right tune.

My Own South American

So maybe Baby, if I'd been a poet at that time I could write
Leaning into the afternoons I cast my sad nets
towards your oceanic eyes... *

But I'd never share it with you, you'd roll your eyes and
laugh, say don't take the piss, and lean back on the veranda
rail smoking.
But in 1969 I didn't know who Neruda was, only that you
were every beat of my heart and each afternoon I'd be on
that veranda waiting, with a disgruntled sun sinking into
the Berbice river.

Leaning into the afternoons

waiting for my river-man.
The carrion crows would laugh from the wires and Mr
Phillips
pounded his piano keys, drown the sound of children
warbling
raw notes into the air.
I would have changed three times: the white pedal-pusher
jeans
the new pink mini-skirt, the chain belt, that lemon frock
you liked with the peepholes...

Leaning into the afternoons

cupping my chin till my elbows slipped,
reliving each yesterday's plunder of my mouth,
each cigarette and Old Spice taste,

each forbidden passage of my navigating fingers
And I waited for the whistle from the street below, the
rattle at the gate, and in one cool twist of my seersucker
waist I would become
Hayley Mills or Funicello and never in a million years

let on how each waiting minute had been a million deaths
and by that time the night had dropped by
and I could only read your lips by the fireflies.

*Pablo Neruda

Soon, Baby, Soon

Hilda pleased the man with kisses
promises of babies, cooked and entertained
held her head high in the street

Soon, Baby, soon, he whispered
passing shop windows where gold rings gleamed
and confetti gathered like guests

The new house beamed, the Cadillac
loitered in the drive, trips to Martinique
to voodoo women, love shots in the rum

Then the belly bore fruit, moonshine
and starshine children, coral crisp
and cornflake children running in the drive

The kisses ceased to taste of oleander
breast milk turned his stomach
a flatter stomach turned his head.

***

Hilda holds her head high in the street
the pram holds her belongings, moonshine
children tread behind her in the dust.

Quarter-done, Half-done, All-done

My Momma washing her hand in cold water
lean on sink
she remembering me, water come ah she eye
> don't cry Momma
> quarter-baby still here
> singing in the sting of your skin

My Dadda pat Momma belly, kiss she
they choosing name fuh me
Francis, Bernadette ...
they say whole rosary, but me still cyant stay
> don't cry Momma
> half-baby still here
> singing in the sting of your skin

Room fulla Doctor and Priest
they wrap me in cotton-wool
nobody must touch me
Momma pon the white sheet too
I's her little Saviour
we going down the road together
> don't cry Dadda
> Momma safe wid me
> we's all done now
> singing in the sting of your skin, my Dadda
> we singing in the sting of your skin

Caribbean Lullaby

On the morning of my memory
Momma rocks me on a hammock slung
between two trees and her brownskin knees
        singing, 'Coconut child, my palm-nut baby
        tamarind sweet
        my sugarcane pickney'

In the noon-time of my memory
my Dadda is playing blues guitar
sleek and wet like a calabash gourd
        singing, ' Coconut child, my palm-nut baby
        tamarind sweet
        my sugar-cane pickney'

In the twilight of my memory
fireflies dance in the kerosene lamp
and the moon smiles down and the stars shine down
        singing, 'Coconut child, my palm-nut baby
        tamarind sweet
        my sugar-cane pickney'

Now this is an English lullaby
my coconut child, my palm-nut baby
tamarind sweet, my sugarcane pickney
Momma rocks you in your memory of ...

Hey Baby

Emeralds darling, always.

Matched my eyes, they said
Like the mists over Roraima
Proper lickle kiskadee
In her seersucker dan-dans!
Baby madam feathers flying
When she stamp her lickle foot nuh!

And they chortling
And filling up the glasses quick-quick
With rum.

And latuh, y'know
Bald Mendonza prospecting upriver
Dipping in de Essequibo with he calabash
And motor-boat –
Bring me back a lickle nugget y'know
Dangle it on my neck
With he fat fingers and bush rum breath.

'I gon kyatch you a emerald next time round
Promise, sweet thing!'

So yes, well
Time ah pass, as they say.
But yuh see these eyes?
They still the same colour y'know. True-true.

Reculver

A hush is still apparent
Even as walkers' children test
Their echoes against the wind
And dogs on leads strain
After elusive scents
Sacredness stands testament

It's roots like sycamores' snake
Not only into constantly eroding soil
But into consciousness –
Grabbing at posterity
And in its austerity
Commanding land and sea

The hungry channel pounds
Tide by tide against its buttressed sides
Still greedy to recover
A sacred Reculver
Whose square-thumbed towers jut
A victory sign into the sky.

Blessings

(1)

Blessed be children and grandchildren, clutter in my front
room
Blessed be forty year-old sisters still borrowing frocks and
shoes
Blessed be my mother and her Tesco's carrier bag
Blessed be my lover swapping red wine for fags
Blessed be girlfriends especially those who cook
Blessed be fellow writers, always plugging their books
Blessed be sunshine, a Caribbean fable
Blessed be ready meals from microwave to table
Blessed be holidays, gypsies on the hoof
Blessed be rain pinging on the conservatory roof
Blessed be this island, my South Coast retreat
Blessed be this England where I landed on my feet.

(2)

Angie
in the kitchen with a frying pan
olive oil and garlic, steam rising
sautéed prawns gliding into
Meringue and Samba.
The memory's there in the dancing flesh
an inheritance of mangoes ripening
in Guyana sun.
My first-born girl, heart as wide
as that continent she's never seen.

(3)

Eloise
holding her son out to me
mirth rippling from the corners
of her mouth, her eyes
questions dancing.
An Odette body
still lean enough for Vogue and Elle
brunette hair spring-water smooth
burnished Welsh river stones,
feet one hundred miles above the floor

(4)

Fifteen, I remember Fifteen ...*
There are new boys waiting at the gate
bolder, eyes full face
tracking Aimee's magic scent, her braided hair
her long tanned legs.
They come sniffing like wild dogs
and we wait at the battlements
ready to shoot them down
grind their necks down into the earth
with our hob-nailed boots.
Instead we smile like Norman Bates
and sing, *Please come in*
she won't be long.

*from 'Fifteen', *Limbolands*

(5)

The grandchildren have been, bless them
tiny Polly Pocket people crunch like snails
on the laminate floor, Lego lorries skateboard
Grand-dad and me into the wall and each other.
The darlings. The cat is clawing desperately
at the sun-bonnet it's wearing, the dog's
chewing at chocolate spread hair-bobbles on her tail;
the dolls are lined up on the settee like Chuckie
waiting; we're afraid to lift them, there are teeth
behind those smiles and blue eyes follow us
as we move.
The children have had a wonderful time,
tumblers of orange squash lie drunkenly
in front of the telly, the video's playing Dalmatians
(again) and popcorn gleams like fool's gold
from corners of cushions and rims of plant pots.
We beam at each other: how fortunate we are!
And how we love to see them

go.

The Recipe

My Dear Daughter,

I hope this finds you well. As you can tell
Included is your birthday card, I wish you all God's blessings
Although as we all know, life is hard.

Well Child, you are so far away I pray
This reach you safe, for as you know
They thiefing anything these days.
But thanks, I got the money that you wrap up in the note.
Good thinking girl, using that past-it's-best envelope.

I been racking my brains to create
Something different for you to celebrate
And minding that lil Patrice you say
Only like Macdonald's food and microwave,
Thought I'd pen to paper that recipe you always aksing for.

For Pepperpot you will definitely need
Some Casryp, that is the main ingredient,
Real Amerindian Guyanese Casryp.
But before you get on your ricketics
Aunt Lollie daughter Fay just get her ticket
She flying out sometime end of May.

The next important is the meat, should be beef
But though we both know more mad cow
Does walk the road on two leg never four
You could substitute that English lamb or pork.

You really needing salt beef, pigtail, cow heel too
Don't turn you nose up, I hear bird flu is the next thing
Sent to try us but never mind, find garlic, thyme
And plenty pepper: bird pepper black pepper

Or Pepper sauce. Rub up, leave to marinate.

While that doing, did I mention Father Gabriel died?
His sister wrote and told me. Poor man, he
Baptise all you girls, he'd roll up in his grave
If he knew y'all girls don't see Church inside.

I personally would leave that meat for two/three hour
But times have changed and you busy being both
A working wife and mother. All that time I rocked you
In Ma chair, who thought you'd settle halfway round the world?!

Next take it out the soak, fry well with onion
Till it brown then add casryp and water, and always taste!
Pepperpot will tell you when he ready, and remember
That dish always taste better the next day!

Well my child, with this recipe I send my warmest love.

Always,

Your loving Mother.

To the Lady's Slipper Orchid, a Daughter

To the Lady's Slipper Orchid, a daughter.
But this time she breathes in glass jars
Teased into life by gloved hands
Fragile with the memory of plunder

A special propagation, her small seeds settle
Fighting for breath.
Eleven years, they say,
She took to flower.

And I remember Lorraine, and all those babies lost
Regardless of prayers, whole benedictions
Tiny bodies wrapped in cotton wool...

Did her ears too, press low into the sheets
Listening to murmurs of approaching feet...?

This is a strange love
Propelled by the urge to possess and protect
Re-position in time and place
Victorian gardens, foster homes, cold frames

Eleven years, they say, she took to flower

Could that reluctance be
Some memory of sisters, aunts, mothers
Dancing on a hillside
Such flaunting and proliferation of beauty

Direly paid for,
A lady's slipper cupped
Into the palm of a protector?

To the Lady's Slipper Orchid, a daughter.
Eleven years, they say, she took to flower

(title from *The Independent*, 18th September 2000)

No Lady

Ladies' voices tinkle through the yard
Jacob, sweep up the leaves, you hear?
Their high heels click up the front steps
Dawdle there

Children skate their bike wheels through the rain.

Women climb the backsteps
De-bone mullet, sever heads
Flesh their voices loud
In the Caribbean air

Children skate their bike wheels through the rain.

But when the Banks Beer pour
Ladies' knees go slack, fall apart
And women's laughter straight and true
Bursts over the heads of children

Skating their bike wheels
Feet on handlebars
Through the rain.

Paradise Fruit

St. Lucia?
Walcott drew me there
essays later. Fretwork balconies
the boy returning, Anna,
Castries burning.

We found the beach near Cap Estate
the tropical dream, surf pounding
wide-leafed trees who dropped
their golden fruit like Topaz.

I am not a tourist. I
am a Guyana woman re-emerging.
Here, I tell my lover and my child
y'all try this, dounze from back home

we had a tree big big by we back door.
I take the first bite, palms
and jewels glinting, say, is all right
this is Paradise, and from up high

birds laughed and cracked their short beaks
on the bark where loose messages
flap: Do Not Sit Beneath Do Not Eat.
Our mouths begin to burn.

Shame drops through my bones
I am become Snow White's mother,
Eve.
Take this, here is my body. Eat.

From Gros Islet to Castries Hospital
Francis the taxi driver reassures us
no-one's died. Ushers us
through patients waiting, heads curled

like question marks round doorways
incredulous at tourists
eating manchineel.

My daughter's screams are louder than the surf
rivalling the scratching of this poet's pen.
Is it a folly then, this tale, these words
that fashion beauty out of pain?

Lament to a Dead Cockerel

You posed for our photograph like tourists
Your brother in your wake, heads high
Combs outlined against the ginger lilies

I knelt to centre you within the lens
Red cockscombs on blue St Lucian skies
White whips of wild clouds spinning

Cacti spines cut across your horizon
Flesh fat against the white palings
Your head, cocked to the side, filling the frame

You escorted us like ushers, up the steps
Past terracotta pots, guava and banana trees
Conch shells cemented into the concrete

In the early mornings you cut into our sleep
With your cacophonous chorus, early risings
With the sun over Rodney Bay

And we linger on the balcony, watching
The yachts on the marina, the hummingbird
Busy in the ivy in the mid-morning sun

Then you again, but this time an angry squawking
You, gripped tight in a fist, disappearing
Through the doors of the restaurant

In the photograph you fill the frame
Head cocked to one side, red cockscomb on blue St Lucian
sky
And wild whips of white clouds, spinning.

Sugar

sugar... water for shock
sugar... bags in Gopaul shop
sugar... sail South China Sea
sugar... sweeten Indian tea
sugar... smooth little Padraic hair
sugar... stalks stabbing the air
sugar... crumbs, Granny table, ants
sugar... cake, flambeaux lamps
sugar... cane, verdant green
sugar... coating, polio vaccine
sugar... baby, Rosetti locks
sugar... daddy, Yves St Laurent frocks
sugar... sweet Margie Riley singing
sugar... still, rum vat rippling
sugar... lump melting on tongue
sugar... trash, black rainfall over town

... water for shock

Aunt Tita

Caught fire she did, straight up
Kero stove, long nightie, old
perfect combo really, considering
the wicker and the drapes
the mahogany love-seat polished to glass

Dee caught a glimpse of her face
from our upstairs window *contorted*
she said, as they wheeled her
in the ambulance and couldn't resist
taking a poke at me always refusing to kiss her

we all get old child, you'll see
but all that mahogany and brass
didn't marry up with the smell
of Limacol and camphor
and her Johnson's skin thin and blue like litmus

could never imagine her sat there
with Mr T. him in his courting suit
and her in organza like the photo
back to back smooching; too late now
and even watching our Dee cry felt like shit

for asking,
the love-seat, did that go too?

... bags in Gopaul shop

Recently he had developed a fear of tall buildings.
Retirement had been good, a piece of real estate
in the Washington suburbs, quiet neighbours, golf course nearby.

Of course it wasn't the same, what was?
He had been a Big Man; Chief Accountant,
shaker of hands with Prince Phillip, Carter, Castro.

He missed the life, wouldn't deny it;
seeing the old city glide past the tinted windows
the dark glasses of the black chauffeur .

He'd done well for a *coloured* man, instilled that
into his kids and hadn't he been proved right?
All living well in NJ and Toronto except the girl

who wouldn't listen and went for that black boy instead.

He watches his wife move slowly
round the kitchenette preparing a little home food
to whet his appetite.

Had she known about the others? The little secretaries
squealing on the mahogany desk
the Canadian wife going down on him between courses?
Denise in the house by the seawall...?

Of course he loved his wife, dammit.
And He was still Big. Showed the relatives round Manhattan,
Staten Island, Lady Liberty, The World Trade Centre.

And now his grand-daughter wanting to
research our history, Poppa... picking at scabs
with her University pen.

How had he come to this?
From scooping those glorious grains in his grandfather's shop
to his flourished signature across the Atlantic, all the way
to Tate and Lyle.

Now viewing the world through a TV screen
his wife dropping a saccharine tab into his tea,
he could almost feel himself dissolving.

... sail South China Sea

(*Gap Year*)

She watched her boy go
disappear into a July morning
off a grey tarmac

he wouldn't wait for his results
I'm going Mum, whatever
I've a lifetime for mortgages and all that crap

Emails arrived from Shanghai, Thailand
digital photos of her brownskin boy smiling
Wicked here Mum! People fantastic!

In September a postcard from Bali
You'd love it here! Staying on for a bit.
Like the card? She looks like you!

Kali's arms are dancing
her eyes red jewels
in black stone.

... smooth little Padriac's hair
(for Eileen Sheehan)

O Eilish ni ...
Once your poems were growing
shorter and shorter so
I feared they'd disappear completely
off the page

until I figured out
you'd woven them so tightly
only mothers could read them
or daughters dream them

and how tightly you'd seamed them
from scalp to coast
hiding the words so cleverly
they metamorphosed.

... stalks stabbing the air

I got to hold on to this brownskin man tight
if is fuck he want is fuck he gon get
lie down in that hammock there or upstairs
when Mummy gone out he knocking back the rum
laughing knowing how he kisses sweet and deep
and fingers in my panties teasing rivers
I never knew was there

I got to hold on to this whiteskin man tight
he like to shag me by the kitchen sink
say hold on there baby let me see
that pussy dark and wet open nice for me
your smell sure drive me wild intoxicate
it must be all that sunshine in your blood
sweet, o sweet jesus so sucking sweet

... crumbs, Granny table, ants

Cora's shopping list includes:

Bleach
Asda special kitchen cleaner
Frish worktop spray with anti-bacterial agent
Ajax scouring powder, fly swat
Fragrance spray, sponges, wire scrubbers, mops
Rubber gloves, plug-in sprays, humidifier
Scented candles, anti-tobacco aerosols
Vapona fly-spray, ant-killer
Woolworths Spray for Flying and Crawling Insects
Blue toilet cubes, joss-sticks
Lifebuoy soap, deep-pore cleanser
Anti-perspirant, Pond's cold cream
Brillo pads, Sanitix, toilet duck
Jeyes Fluid
Bleach

This might be London, but, as Cora says,
Living in the tropics prepares you.

... flambeaux lamps

recently there has been a rise in carnival processions
a water-water mix of multiculture
street parades have become the thing, lanterns
inflame the night-time sky, the English know at last
that victory parades and carnival are one and the same
and artists are doing very well, thank you

fanfare and Halloween, Diwali yes please
Yemanja banners blazing from Brazil
grace Canterbury City streets whilst
her sister Mary working
the day shift in the Cathedral

In Broadstairs Anansi mingles merrily with Morris Men
and djembe drummers lead the Torchlight to the sea
whilst Lewes crowds are warned to stay away because
the price of all this pleasure means we're unleashing

all our festive dreams and now there's cautions
of the problems of policing.
But if this island's lungs have trouble breathing
is that not the true-true spirit
of Carnival?

... verdant, green

you look at me and see a cube of sugar honey
even come up close and tek a taste
find it oh so sweet

is true, cane pretty, tall and swaying in the breeze
you can go trekking
have piknik by a likkle stream

but hold dis cube o sugar baby
under the nostrils just so
tek a sniff before you melt me
on your tongue or stir me
in your tea

you smell dat smell honey?
dat hint o black molasses dere
dat trace dat does make the rum burn hot
and dot you tongue with fire?

you close enough to taste salt
close enough to imagine me curl up
in a ball at your feet
under your machete?

you look at me and see a cube o sugar honey
but sweet only know sweet
when it taste bitter

... coating, polio vaccine

so this is the time when this stuff get serious

all the time I carried you
like a ship we sailed
rolling as the months went by
cocooned against the waves
we only took the best on board
fresh fruit and eggs, fish
a little organic meat

then the winds came
and whipped you from me
screaming above the gales
and here we are
marooned on land
compass as slack
as a used rubber band

so I bring you here today trusting
that these things they tell me are true
that the stuff in these needles will protect you
this small cube of sugar keep you safe
and you'll run and you'll play
and you'll dance and you'll sing
as I once did
as I once did

forgive me my darling, my innocent dear
you're no longer on board, I no longer steer

... baby, Rossetti locks
... sugar daddy, Yves St Laurent frocks
(for Dorothea)

Dear Lizbeth dear, Dear Jane Siddal,
Dear Ava, Vivienne, Scarlett, Marilyn,
Or any o'yall out there

We dreamt of you and your tresses
Back-combed, pressed, tonged and curled
Stitched and stitched in the burning heat
To re-create your dresses

I was my Daddy's princess
Baby, never cut your hair
So lucky, didn't need hot combs
Was pale, *half-way there!*

But listen Daddy, my Daddy dear
They say long hair is aging
Though my heart still beats at the thought of boys
And a house in the Mediterranean

The lady is waiting, her scissors sharp
And I'm reading Jean Rhys, *Voyage in the Dark*
Been to the Tate but leave confused
With tales of bricks and beds and sugar

So dahlings all I'll join you
Down the road of myth and mist
No sugar-baby any mo,
Just lickle ole lickle ole *me*

... sweet Margie Riley singing

to the hills of Kerry these goblin men they come
to Dingle Bay and Innisfree they come
to Dublin's fair city, to Galway and Cork
to Clare and Shannon and right through the North
they come

they're sweetening our children these goblin men they are
they're buying our houses these goblin men they are
they're dealing in euros, in dollars and yen
dribbling white powder from the Pied Piper's den
from the rock of ages to the golf course
here they come

but in a clear light on a good day
in a clear light on a good day
the singing of Margie Riley reaches out
and over the sound

... still, rum vat rippling

Barbados in the rain, the Malibu factory
We clamber up hot steel to view the still fermenting
And I see her face reflected, that young girl missing
Since last Thursday, her body found in the cane-field

I can't bear to think of her running from him
Scorpions and centipedes, the cane rat, her bare feet
The hard scratch of the leaves, the chocolate earth
Her blood seeping down into limestone

Did she beg him not to leave her there, with all those ghosts?
Did the cane stretch their young necks for a glimpse of her throat?

My daughter taps impatiently, her corn rows neat
Holiday beads swinging as she moves
The rain stops
The air is still

... lump, melting on tongue

Ah ain't gonna do it. Shant
Ah's sick to death of counting every fucking calorie
Don't care what they say
Ain't the women he met no longers anyway

Ah've tried ma best – reduced the eggs
Swapped butta fuh low fat shit
Startuhs for desserts. Can't remember
Last time ah chomped a steak.
And that's anodder thing, ma teef.

Can't read no mo, don't want to read
It's all crap anyways an TV only Ophrah's
Worth the license fee and then
Only wiva cappuchino and cinnamon waffle
Double cream

Dressing up?
What's the point?
Ain't going nowheres plus
The Doc he's coming fix me up wiva
bigger chair any day now

No oddah fucker comes 'cept him
and he don't count. As fuh the Boy
he gwine long time, the cunt.

So let me be. And No.
Ah'm nevuh giving up the sugar in ma tea.

... trash, black rainfall over town

They've killed the dentist
the news is on the internet
pictures of his wife
clutching a neighbour
crying as if her life depended on it

It was the bandits they said
strange words bandits but
this is South America and
before sugarcane stretched
from here to Brasilia
plenty bandits roamed this way
Columbus, conquistadores ...

But this was no way to end it
gunned down
in his own surgery
on a foreday morning
his wife asleep upstairs

Remnants of my first teeth lie
somewhere in that red soil
and the beginnings of my fear
lie back and open wide, this won't hurt
but you could hear the screaming
right across Main Street.
He slapped my sister once.

He'd had the chance to leave,
his son begged him from America
Get out Dad, but no
this was Home
this small mosquito strip of coast
within the shadow of the cane
which fell
when the fields burned
like black rain

he farmed chickens on the Corentyne Coast
the first to freeze them
stored them in his garage
behind the surgery
a daring venture amongst country people
who bought their fowls live and fattened them
in their own backyards while the children whined
Ma don't kill she, we don't want eat she

But of course we would
fowl curry taste good
and our country's history groomed us well
in paradox, the bible and the cane.

Still, he shouldn't have died that way
sugar-sweet blood seeping
into the soil
into the thin crowing
of a fowl-cock morning

Conch

Conch dripping salt water turn his belly to the sun
Conch singing of the joys of life
Conch twist in the surf bounce up high on the waves
Conch tangle up with fishing line
Conch shouting at the top of his voice but nobody
hear
Conch scream, brothers, is not my time!

Conch simmering in a stew pot dreams of the
Atlantic
Saturated in cooking oil and garlic.

Meditation

that bird singing outside that window
early bird, late bird
bird dreaming of fandango
late night soirees on some veranda

he is remembering St Lucia, the Antilles
a fisherwoman's ballad of the sea
light is streaming through her net
net full of singing sardines

and a hot mouth conch thinking
he's the business but who
later that day becomes lambi
for 60 EC dollars down by the waterfront

where the cruise ships slide easy into blue

HOTEL ROOMS

The George, Colchester

There is some joy in a woman entering a hotel,
some spring in the step, glory in waltzing up a wide staircase
key dangling from her hand.

Today Room 105 is mine. Not as glam as 101 but it'll do.
Soon you'll be here and will speak of motorways, the aunts,
the garden centre;

and listen to my day, of artists from South India, Jamaica
and Ghana all celebrating the end of one project
and planning another,

and how, interspersed between notions of Stereotype and
Inter-culture
were cups of coffee, pastries, chicken tikka sandwiches
and dips, and my own lunchtime wandering

into Zanzibar, from where my new cotton trousers,
embroidered bag and incense
now claim this indeterminate space
mine.

＊＊＊

To Zanzibar and back in one long day.
I wait for you in 105 stretched out on the duvet.

Voyeur

Don't ask me to get undressed, shower
become, at the click of your finger, a femme fatale.

I need warming, like a large slow stone in the sun,
Kneading, like bread on the rise.

No. Bring me your body,
lay it out before me, my request.
I'll be the voyeur, you the guest.

Prested Hall
March 03

Frost is on the willow
silvering her arms down to the lake
where blond reeds rise
from a water matt with mist.

At dawn, geese had called
up to this window framed
by a lattice of lead. Now
a wood pigeon squats through the lift

of your breathing.

They say the war has started.
Hard to believe that here, where the mirror
in the French Armoire reflects only
white sheets and your head still

on the pillow.

Last night the car had nosed
through the fog, creeping
Lord of the Rings country
a landscape on night-watch marking

our slow passage.

And here we were: an entrance door
suitably creaking, a lone proprietor

guiding us up past oak banisters,
a long 16th century corridor.

Only now can I see the lake,
the wooden bridge, flat farmland
with footpaths leaking into the morning.

This is the first hotel I have seen
real coffee on the Welcome tray;
never mind I don't drink it,
it's good to know that it's there.

They say the war has started.
Right now, in this borrowed space
it's this minuscule peace
I hold near.

The Scheregate Hotel

So this is Independence. This small room
with patterned quilt, no view, a bathroom
gurgling through a midnight wall
a dark-stained door that sticks.

I'm in a foreign land, fake Tudor land.
A half-empty train spat me out at Colchester Town
into a right-turn left-turn just past the roundabout dear
straight up St John's Street.

My small case trolleyed behind me.
I was born in St John's Street
New Amsterdam, Guyana
Number 20

In 1971 landed just up the road at Stansted
hippy and lipsticked
and ready for The World.
Full circle.

No evening meals, so I brave the town centre
before dusk, take away chicken 'n chips
return like a rat to my nest. Call home
from beneath the sheets, the TV

a friendly eye by the Welcome Tray.
The bathroom gargles all night.
Footsteps creak, doors slam.
Dawn curls slowly through the curtains

into a morning stinking of chips which I cram
guilty into the wastebasket, open the window
to a cold crisp day above the drainpipes.

In the breakfast room there's a toaster
on each table. Full Breakfast please,
with poached.

I meet the eyes of the lone woman at table 3,
small smiles cross over the rim of our tea.
So this, is Independence.

The Penguin Hotel

I remember you well in the Penguin Hotel
bare arms warm on the sill
a breeze from the river invisibly lifting
the damp black hairs of your skin

I'd returned to find you and find you I did
in Water Street waiting, a beer in your hand
and the sun beat down on me and my lies
the sun beat down on my lies

I remember you well in the Penguin Hotel
in a pale green shirt and blue jeans
your dark hair falling over your eyes
I'd returned with another man's child

Returned with another man's child
and we wept, for the years we had lost
and the sun beat down on me and my lies
the sun beat down on my lies

The hotel's day was gone like ours
paint peeling away in the heat
but the girls still limed in the wide alleyway
still dressed up to the nines

Once Mercedes cars had purred past the doors
and fat cats lounged by the bar
in tangerine slacks and Guyana gold
business meetings kept on hold

for the sole pursuit of pleasure.

Someone begged for a cigarette –
fifty cents for the jukebox,
you angry that your hands were shaking –

The Eagles singing
Hotel California right through the pores of our skin.

An old man slammed his dominoes down
into the mouth of our breathing
and the sound beat down on me and my lies
the sound beat down on my lies

I remember you well in the Penguin Hotel
that sun slinking away
into the river I'd crossed for you
and which haunts me still

your bare arms dark as you held me still
in a room at the Penguin Hotel

Hotel Trebeurden
Brittany '03

I guess from the upstairs balcony you can see the sea
But we've French doors and gravel and white plastic chairs

The girl was pretty, and our eyebrows talked
Of important things like the bill and whether breakfast was
included

The Brittany School is represented on the wall
Indigo and cobalt, ochre triangular sails (one M. Jean
Duquoc)

The Euros had been reluctant to leave my palm, dreaming
perhaps
Of Bordeaux or that fine necklace back in Pont Aven with
the blue stones

Just think, yesterday in Morlaix I almost bought
Yet another Gauguin postcard

The Lake Hotel, Killarney

The Magillycuddy Reeks above us in the rain.
One year later, we're here again

trying not to be tourists. This time we've the grand seats
but the view's the same,

the short walk down to Lough Leane
the faerie castle, the trees

where the children found a photo torn in two,
a woman and child smiling.

The Americans have gone but the Russians are here
sprawled in the Punch Bowl Tavern

Glasnost and Guinness leather-jacketed
against the chrome. We're thinking of home

but our words remain where they originate –
in that rough curl of the throat where the heron

rises from the mist and etches
its low soundless flight across the lake.

Leaving

Leaving Ballylongford that Sunday
I thought of you. Thought of you
through the wind and rain
driving me back along the Shannon
and away

You had not stirred when I left
a restless night had your limbs askew
like a new foal angled
against the field of your sleep
your lips pressing into the pillow

There would be no tomorrow, this I knew
and wondered, hours later
what time you had woken
and whether you had found that small gift
curved beneath your breast

like a swallow

Go West, Young Woman

And there I am reading poetry
In O'Carrol's bar, Ballylongford
The new girl in town
And amongst the whispers and the craic
I'm watching the door swinging
Like the Last Chance Saloon
Waiting for that moment when your head appears
Like Gary Cooper and you'll pause for one long moment
And thumb your hat off your forehead
And pin us all to the wall with your steel blue eyes
And if you don't appear
Only I will know that the hoss
Must have stumbled somewhere on the N17
His 1971 VW heart coughing that
He just don't do hooves
Hombre.

Martini Girls

1976. And me and my baby are riding the train
Her curled to my belly, warm on my thighs
And the train hiccups through Dover, skims
For one surreal moment along the track
With the sea to our left and a bright sun swimming
On an emerald sea.
                Then the tunnels
And a force-fed wind screaming its anger
At our freedom to move through its confined space
And I'm moving my fingers to cover her ears
Her sweet baby four-month ears, remembering
The classics, the occasional Bob Marleys
The dancing with her still wrapped in my belly.

Folkestone. And me and my baby meet Emily
(we'd worked at the factory), she's wheeling her baby
I'm carrying mine, the sun's shining bright
And we're warped in delight at our beauty
21(ish) real hair, good teeth, breasts fulsome
To whistles, oestrogen dripping and both of us wearing
The dresses we'd made,
                Martini labels on black, on red
Backless, shoulder less, full-skirted pretend Monroes
Teased into being our mothers (but cool) with trips
(before childbirth) to Jap and Joseph and Anyone
in the Fulham Road.
Sun hot on our heads we paraded our babies
Along Capel le Ferne. Watched the sea, swelled fatter
And fatter as The World and His Wife took time off

From strolling to peer at our babies and croon
How like their mothers they were
And they don't stay babies for long, enjoy.

2001. And this memory rises as I ride on the train
And I think of my baby, now 25,
And her babies and Emily's babies
And Emily and wonder what happened
What happened to those

Frocks?

'... the child, tiny and alone,
creates the mother.'
>
> Adrienne Rich

You are mine and mine only
My cherry-red hot air balloon
Lifting me from an Atlantic bath
Into an English sky

We sideways step into double-decker buses
Roll into Tescos like a steamship
Importing cargo. Your okra fingers
Juck my belly, point to the full fat ice-cream
Viennese whirls, microwave pizzas
Liquorice sticks.

I am yours and yours only
In our midnight feasts Daddy sleeps through
Our calypso while cocoa butter anoints
The messages you're marking on my skin

I want to keep you here
My passageway, my roadmap
My new tongue, my street light
I'm holding on tight tight to the string

Calling

You're gone. A voice at the end of the line frizzling into
night rushing to ring off as usual (you never have any credit
and only have time to say what you phoned for)
I'm left cradling plastic and remembering the smell of you
all Johnson's baby and breast milk then later Charles Lauren
and I'm wondering how come time moved so fast from
when I first held a telephone – Uncle Bert's black Bakelite –
1966 age 12 before my own migration and the mystery
never left, telephones and radios and how come a voice can
crawl on cables underneath the ocean and what's all that
stuff about sound waves and now satellites and look mum
no hands smaller and smaller mobiles
And now I'm thinking how quickly the words 'I'm mobile'
become 'immobile' with the removal of an apostrophe,
remembering how you dropped your h's as quick as your
skirt rose, as quick as your new high boots would allow
And I think of you now in some city whose name I'm not
allowed to know, no longer linked by blood but stars and
the mystery returns that absence of touch
cutting into my flesh like cheese wire.

August Rains

Don't you know I love you, my August girl?
My belly was as big as this swollen sky
That threatens to burst with rain

These are dark days, and I tremble with the pain
Of losing you, deserting you in some strange room
Where you pace incognito

Believe, believe
Come rain, come shine, I will wait for you
                              And wait
                              And wait
                              And wait

Alice Falling

she falls she falls
and in her dreaming
great protuberances
of continents
dangle their
bleached limbs
down
through the
chocolate earth

she falls she falls
and in her falling
The Atlantic roars above her
like bathwater
and great shoals of herrings
rush
past her feet

she falls she falls
this falling is like waltzing
a current cups her
like a hammock
lowering her
down down
on fat slings of air

her head can swivel like an owl's
her arms are gladly scratched
by the toenails of elms kicking
into nothingness

she falls she falls
red petals of hibiscus
lighting the way
raining confetti
Chinese lanterns of welcome
an entire city waiting
far far below
for her landing

The Crypt, St Nicholas-at-Wade, Birchington

The Thanet Way whistles into the distance
Sarre Windmill turns; in the orchard
Sun-browned children play amongst the sunflowers

The house nestles into trees
Windows and white walls light a path breathing
In a memory of horse-riders

We are welcomed, guided
Along a flag-stoned floor, an opening
Downwards, a black descent

The children had placed nite-lites
On each step, and our hands sought
The damp walls, following all those footsteps ...

Then the crypt, fanning into four corners
Bricked candlelit recesses, cathedral ceiling
Tales of Huguenots, Cromwell, smuggled wine

Priests' bodies barely breathing, pressed close
Swallowing sacraments silently
In the dim light of tallow

This last we carry outside
Blinking at the four-wheel-drives,
The cold dust of stone on our soles.

Samphire Hoe

A new piece of England, I
glinting at your feet
phosphorescent in this light
this dazzle of wind, sail, wing

Too long did I lie in the deep
some Sycorax tossing
heartbeat shallow to sunken masts
listening awake for the promise

But here now, am I
turning to the sky's embrace
open to the sun's glare
the skein of tyre tracks

your solid bouncing shoes.
And my gills swell with vision
and skin and hair and teeth
ask, England, England?

Samphire Hoe, a new piece of land between Dover and Folkestone created by
the residue of the Channel Tunnel

Walking the Block With My Cat

It's 3 o'clock in the morning and we're walking the block
you running on ahead, your white tail tipping the darkness
on walls and fences, pausing for me to catch up

There was a full moon earlier, it hung over the sea at Viking Bay
and everyone remarked on it looking out of the big bay
windows
where the birthday party was in full swing

with the Irish guys and all fiddling away into the night.
We can't believe you're 50 that's what they all said but
I feel it in my bones 50 years of walking concrete and earth

tip-toeing, running, tripping up, slouching, kicking out
heels powdered on Caribbean dust and English concrete
this Broadstairs with its ice-cream parlours and cold sand.

Now I'm walking the block with my cat, running away
from all those tears and children's arms and wine-cracked
voices
slurring their insecurities into my pacing, remembering

a year ago this birthday I buried another cat, run down
on the eve of my 49th and out in the garden February daffodils
are already springing up where we buried her.

So where's the joy in any of it, what do we really celebrate
time passing or that to come, looking forward, looking back
it's all the same, there's only this one moment where thoughts

run on like the clicking of this keyboard, the piano keys of our time, and that bastard backdrop moon smirking as our pawed and high-heeled feet turn unwillingly into the front path.

Somewhere a Country and a Lover

So here we are
Kent, England 2004
and the clock's ticking like her inelegant heart

between the beats neat peeps of lovers and small feet
and a shoreline melting with red tears

they're lined up like ducks in a fairground
waiting for the rifles of her fingers
so sweet, *Oh Honeyyy!*

and she's young and so blonde in that dark country
where moustached men brought out their guitars
leaning into the afternoons

her own South American left for Washington
and his little she drummed her fingers on the backs
of European men, seeking her continent in their eyes

in all the barstools in all the world you had to walk into this one

but then all those movies, and Mr Neruda said it all so nice
y'know, all dese words she felt inna her lickle heart
and she slips between registers climbin' zat ladder ova
lurve

listening to *Il Postino* whilst hoovering and mopping the
laminate floor

them words lika molasses slicking 'cross the Atlantic
and she pour them on she Hovis toast
slow slow, from a teaspoon

Praise Song to an Island

Can I call you Home, now, Island?
Island, whose necklace of water is but a memory
Beads in the psyche, a reluctant conjoin to the hip.
Strangers come astray here, settle as if by accident
They come looking for the horizon, but the sea
Unsettles them, stops them in their tracks
They can't go back, face the past, all those goodbyes, again.
So they stay, settle, mark superstore incisions into the trail
Of Vikings, Romans, Iron Men, whilst the old
Bend with their backs to the wind, wondering
Were they wise to retire here on a whim, a childhood
Memory of a summer's day in Margate?

This was not my land, I arrived and nested
Spiralling webbed roots downwards into the chalk
Twisting my neck this way and that
For the finger trails of Alice
And the tiny running feet of the White Rabbit.
Behind me the Wantsum shrivels to a stream
And Reculver stands, a frightened maid
Lifting her skirts out of the water.

This was not my land; I arrived and nested
I cling to the cliff edge like a gull
Always with its eye on the horizon

Safe Harbour
(for Steven)

            i am safe in your arms
                    harboured
                    beneath high white cliffs
                    the sea
                    of my heart
                    ripples
                    to the lull of your breathing

you say when you watch me sleeping i make small noises
like seals or a porpoise beached on the rocks   but this i
deny believing i am noiseless in my sleep extinguished like
the last light.   When i turn into the cove of your arms
and paddle your restless back i am not asleep but dreaming
with my eyes wide open and mouth   smiling.

Mary Dancing

Mary rolling back the rug and slipping
Albums outa dem sleeves
Lord Kitchener, Mighty Sparrow
Hot! Hot! Hot! by Arrow

She trying to get we up dancing
Pulling we outa we chairs
But Granny want watch Cliff Richard
And Desiree patting she hair

'Everybody *Hot! Hot! Hot!*' Mary shout
Punching the air with she fingers
The children giggle and watch she wiggle
Caribbean down to the floor

She wukkin up a sweat
And wukkin up a fete
Steven join she with he wine glass
And Michael leave he sausage roll

'Everybody *Hot! Hot! Hot!*' she shout
And this time she get a chorus
And in one quick shake of a duck tail
Everybody join she on the floor

Yonnette remember she can move
Lizzie get down in the groove
Granny take a swig of brandy
And Aimee mix her funk with ballet

Hot! Hot! Hot! and Ethel Road front room
Become Republic Day
Become Water St and Main St
And Mashramani Day
Is Jouvert and Diwali
Masquerade and Phagwah Day
And Mary is the steel band
Mary is the float

'Hot! Hot! Hot!' we shout
And punch we fingers in the air
Go on Mary! Go on girl!
You dancing for we all!
Go on Mary! Go on Girl! You dancing for we all!

39 Steps and Counting

39 steps they said but I counted 78
from East Cliff promenade
concrete and dark under the cliff-face
then through the gap
Stone Bay, and the sea dancing
through a pocket of light

picture Hannay running
looking back over his shoulder
and up to the cold white house,
falling soft on the sand
in the thinnest beam of morning

but this is where we walk the dog
and she noses catching the scent
on the walkway past the chalets
where a barbecue smoulders black on a white sand
with black-backed gulls and curlews wheeling
and a channel ferry skates on the horizon

there is no sign of u-boats
or spies running in suits
only me on the wrong steps at the wrong time

Valentine Birthdays

(for my grandson Kieren 14.2.2001 and my grandmother Angie Brazh, 14.2.1898 - 6.8.1973)

Were you to meet, what would you say?
Between your birthdays more than a hundred years
Five generations, and the Atlantic Ocean
Between her Guyana and your England

Would you call her Mother, like we all did
Rushing to meet her over the bridge
The donkey cart waiting as she paid the driver
Four grand-daughters ecstatic at her arrival?

Would she have travelled down from the Corentyne
Or sailed upriver from Kwakwani
Would she have brought her parrot, her Polly
Or naughty Jack, the capuchin monkey?

I can see you now scrambling for her lap
With your Bob the Builder truck and your Scoobydoo top
And you'd chatter about Shrek and your new DVD
And your gameboy and what's on the telly

And she'd stroke your blond hair, admire
Your blue eyes, say was a blessing, a St Valentine child
A boy-child, after all these girls, but who
Was Scoobydoo and what was telly?

And she might ask you who you were named for,
St Kieren?

And how she was so proud your Mummy name Eloise
Like your great-granny name Eloise and
Did you know her name. Brazh, was Portuguese?

Her family come from Madeira, you know
You think is co-incidence the two of y'all
Share the same birthday? And she'd press
A gold piece in your hand and say

No matter how big the world, how wide the sea
No matter was even a thousand years pass
Family was family, Happy Birthday,
Valentine Boy.

Anansi Hit Broadstairs
An ode to Broadstairs Folk Week

Anansi hit Broadstairs running
all eight feet ringing with bells
a yellow tam pon he dreads
scuttle down the High Street
checking out The Albert, The Rose
the garden at Bombers
then down through the York Gate
slide in the Tartar Frigate

He buying a pint and question the landlord –
'Seh man, I hear something call Folk Week does happen here.
You have my brudders from Africa, Ireland and Hingland
causing hurricane; djembe and clogs, morris and fiddlers
jamming up the town wicked to Kingdom come!?
Man, I ketch boat, bus and plane to land here
but the place so quiet!
Is only sea I hearing –tell me, is lie they lie 'bout
Multiculture and Torchlight Procession?'

The landlord give Anansi another pint and say,
'Mate you late!
Folk Week was last week!'

But ... those who know Anansi know
he always got the last word ...

'Brud, no way Anansi late,
Anansi come early, ready for next year!'

From Berbice to Broadstairs

'You're the only Caribbean I know,' she says
and my tongue rolls back in my throat
'Guyanese,' I whisper, 'Guyanese'.
Guyana, not Ghana.
South America, not Africa.
I am neither a small island girl
Nor am I a region.

Behind me a continent is screaming
through the clipped teeth of conquistadors.
From Berbice to Patagonia
howler monkeys sing
of the black navel of Rainstorm
her emerald belly bleeding.

'We're looking for a black artist
for our Culturally Diverse Project'.
'Potagee', I whisper, 'Potagee.'
Scurvy, yella girl, red girl, white nigger.
Well actually I'm a Berbician,
just follow the smell of sugar.

Beside me an island is bowing
under the weight of memories
– the Wantsum*, Kurdistan
Zimbabwe, Croatia ...
Palms pause above a drum
fingers over strings.

I remember another word for asylum:
The Berbice Madhouse

The digger's chewing up the earth
between Broadstairs and Margate
between Broadstairs and Ramsgate
those stamp-sized cabbage fields
that make us feel distinct
becoming stone and glass and steel
tarmaced shopping precinct,
digger planting concrete embryos
monolithic missiles
where

girlies in their wedge-heeled shoes
flit fast-paced through the H&M store
clicking text messages to their mates next door

Shop, shop, shop till you drop
Love, love Westwood Cross

'Come far?' the taxi driver asks
'Broadstairs', I say
'Berbice', I whisper

Broadstairs where
Long live Bleak House
the jeweller fits gold taps to baths
where Dickensian characters lived and laughed
and come Fridays gob out
'Fuck yous!'
over Harbour Street.

Broadstairs where
house prices still trade
on imagined gentility
strolling on the promenade, admiring the sea
cool coffee bars and incomers from London
plaster artistic impressions on canvases
already breathing their own rhythm
imprinting their own dreams
exhaling the salt of centuries
each high tide snatches
never
to return

But walk down Joss Bay Road
on an early autumn morning
up through the farm to the lighthouse
down to the sand and cliffs
where the English channel charges

stand for a while and dream –

you might just hear a smuggler laugh
or a parakeet scream.

* The Wantsum River originally divided the Isle of Thanet from the rest of Kent.